The Age of Big Data

How Analytics Is Changing Our World

Table of Contents

Chapter 1. Introduction

In an era characterized by a continuous avalanche of data, understanding and harnessing its potential is emerging as a crucial requirement rather than a mere advantage. The Age of Big Data: How Analytics Is Changing Our World, a special report, delves deep into this fascinating development transforming all corners of our modern world. We invite you, regardless of your background or technical expertise, to take a refreshing journey that expounds on the vast universe of data, through the lens of analytics. In a down-to-earth style, it deciphers complex concepts into comprehensible narratives, making the confluence of data analytics, technology, and society an engaging exploration for everyone. This insightful special report takes you into the heart of trends shaping your tomorrow, empowering you to make data-informed decisions, whether in business, policy, or personal life. So, let's step into the age of big data together because knowing is not enough, it's time to understand. Unlock this world by securing your copy of the special report today.

Chapter 2. An Introduction to the Data Deluge

For as long as human history can trace, data has been the fundamental tool to comprehend the world around us. Our ancestors used primitive forms of data to predict the change of seasons, navigate the vast oceans, and understand the night sky. The modern world now finds itself waist-deep in a deluge of data like never before, a development that's both thrilling and terrifying in its possibilities.

Our current environment is experiencing a data explosion that's transforming various industries and sectors — expanding scales, refashioning methods, and redefining outcomes; this is now being economically stylized as the 'Data Deluge.'

2.1. Understanding the Data Deluge

The term "data deluge" signifies the overwhelming flood of data generated every moment from multifarious sources. Thanks to the advent of modern technology, approximately 2.5 quintillion bytes of data are produced every day. To illustrate this colossal figure in more comprehensible terms, imagine filling 10 million Blu-ray discs with data. The resulting stack of discs would stretch the height of the Eiffel Tower!

This overwhelming cascade of data is attributed to our digital activities, including internet browsing, social media interactions, business transactions, scientific research, technological advancements, and much more. Additionally, the ubiquitous Internet of Things (IoT) devices — from our smartphones to our smart fridges — contribute extensively to this data influx by continually logging and uploading information to the grid.

2.2. The Double-Edged Sword

However, this Data Deluge is undeniably a double-edged sword. On one hand, it presents a reservoir of untapped information that, when harnessed correctly, can unlock significant value across various domains. Be it predicting market trends, enhancing customer service, improving healthcare, or even leading national security — data has the potential to revolutionize the way we understand and interact with the world around us.

On the other hand, the sheer volume of data challenges our existing capabilities to capture, store, analyze, and leverage it effectively. The limitations extend to infrastructure, human expertise, privacy, and security. Also, with an ever-increasing amount of redundant, obsolete, or trivial (ROT) data, the challenge lies in distinguishing valuable data from the chaff.

2.3. Data Analytics: Harnessing the Deluge

Herein, Data Analytics emerges as the lifeboat in this flood. By drawing meaningful insights from the raw data, it guides individuals and organizations to make informed decisions and strategic moves. Analytics can sift through massive amounts of data, identify patterns, extract useful information, and provide valuable insights that were previously unthinkable.

Whether it's recognizing shopping habits to customize promotions, identifying disease patterns to better prepare for health risks, or spotting financial frauds in real-time, Data Analytics arms us with actionable insights in this Age of Big Data.

2.4. Rise of the Data-Driven World

In the backdrop of the Data Deluge, we see the world shifting towards data-driven principles. Today, data is not simply about storing and retrieving information; it's about harnessing predictive power, driving strategic decisions, and improving results. Businesses bank on data-driven insights to stay competitive, Governments leverage data to enhance public services, and individuals turn to data to enrich their day-to-day lives.

However, to enable a data-driven world, we need a paradigm shift—it's not merely about possessing data; it's about how one comprehends, interprets, manages, and uses it. The need for honing data literacy, ethical data governance, data privacy, and security cannot be emphasized enough in this context.

2.5. Looking Ahead

As we continue diving deeper into the era of Big Data, our understanding of the 'Data Deluge' is not just about acknowledging its existence; instead, it's about making conscious efforts to harness its potential. Let's not forget, data is only as valuable as our capability to use it.

This relentless wave of data shows no signs of receding—instead, it continues to mount, demanding our attention, understanding, and respect. Therefore, those who can skillfully navigate the Data Deluge will eventually hold the keys to unprecedented progress and prosperity.

In the following chapters, we'll explore how we can transform the daunting face of the Data Deluge into an ally leveraging data science's power. The expedition will take us through enlightening paths of data categorization, the role of AI & ML in analytics, data privacy concerns, future trends, and much more. Buckle up, it is going to be an enlightening journey into the world of data.

Chapter 3. Decoding Data: Beyond the Numbers

Our journey into the realm of data and analytics may well start with the humble number - numbers that we have been trained from an early age to diligently crunch, calculate, and make sense of. However, in the vast, swirling galaxy of big data we quickly discover that these numbers hold an entirely dimension of meaning and potential. They are no longer mere representations of quantities, but each carries a wealth of information, a story, an insight waiting to be uncovered.

3.1. Unveiling the Stories Hidden in Numbers

Data has been described as the new oil of the 21st century. But much like unrefined oil, raw data - represented by numbers - doesn't offer much value on its own. The 'crude oil' of data needs to be refined, interpreted and translated into meaningful, actionable insights. This is where analytics comes into play.

Consider this: every minute, users are sending hundreds of millions of messages on social media, conducting millions of searches on Google, streaming millions of hours of video, and generating unimaginably massive amounts of digital breadcrumbs. Each of these actions gets distilled into a data point – a number.

But beyond the numerical value that gets recorded, each of these data points potentially carries within it the story of who performed the action, when did they do it, how did they do it, and why. The challenge lies in finding ways to extract these stories.

3.2. The Science and Art of Data Analysis

Data analysis in its simplest form can be seen as the process of making the raw data tell its story. Traditional analytical techniques typically employ statistical methods to identify trends or patterns in a collection of data. These often involve calculations of averages, correlations, and regressions, or comparisons of groups using methods such as t-tests, chi-square tests, and the likes.

One might argue that these constitute the 'science' of data analysis. However, the advent of big data has brought the 'art' of data analysis into focus too. With big data providing us with rivers of information, the challenge now is as much about finding meaningful insights from a sea of irrelevant information, as it is about producing statistically sound results.

For instance, modern data scientists use algorithms to learn from high-dimensional data, using machine learning techniques that can uncover complex, non-linear relationships among multiple variables. Visualization techniques present data in highly intuitive and interactive graphical formats, enabling key insights to be gleaned from a glance at a well-constructed chart or diagram.

3.3. Transforming Numbers into Narratives

One critical aspect of data analysis is to turn the numbers into narratives, a form of communication that is universally understood and appreciated. Here, understanding data implies not just extracting statistically significant trends or patterns, but also interpreting these trends in a manner that relates to real world phenomena – in other words, turning numbers into stories.

Modern data analytics tools are capable of identifying the trends and patterns in data, but it is the skill of a data scientist to distill this information into a digestible format for decision-makers. This often involves producing data visualizations, dashboards or reports that communicate the state of affairs in a clear, unambiguous manner.

For instance, a marketing department might wish to know not just which products are selling well, but also who is buying them, when, where, and in response to what promotional strategies. The corresponding analysis might involve correlating sales data with customer demographics, location data, and marketing campaign metrics, and condensing all this information into a single dashboard that tells a cohesive, actionable story.

3.4. Embracing a Data-Driven Future

As we move further into the age of big data, organizations and individuals alike must prepare to harness the power of analytics to unlock the potential held within numbers. This involves not just acquiring skills in using modern data analysis tools and techniques, but also fostering a data-driven culture that values evidence over intuition and instinct.

In conclusion, the process of decoding data – of seeing beyond the numbers – involves a journey of curiosity, exploration, experimentation, and communication. It requires us to understand what the numbers represent, to interrogate them until they yield their secrets, and to communicate these insights in a manner that can guide decision making. As we continue to navigate the age of big data, this skill will only become more valuable.

Chapter 4. The Art and Science of Data Analytics

Data analytics sits at the confluence of various disciplines including mathematics, statistics, computer science, and industry-specific knowledge. This blend of art and science has become central to deciphering the vast stores of digital data produced, stored, and managed every day.

4.1. The Role of Data Analytics in Business

Before we can fully appreciate the power of analytics, it's critical to understand its connection to business. Data analytics allows businesses to gain insights, make better decisions, and predict future trends. Suppose a company is looking to improve customer satisfaction. In this case, data analytics might analyze customer feedback and product data to identify where the issues are. It provides these insights by processing huge volumes of raw data and finding patterns, correlations, and other statistical links.

Using quantitative techniques, analysts can discover meaningful information hiding in plain sight, developing clear business strategies. This is where the blend of artistry and science comes to life. It's not just about numbers and algorithms; data analytics is also about the intuitive ability to see and interpret patterns.

4.2. Tools and Technologies

In the industry today, several tools and technologies aid data analytics. SQL (Structured Query Language) is the backbone of many companies' data operations. SQL allows you to retrieve specific information from large datasets, executing commands such as SELECT, UPDATE, DELETE, and INSERT. Python and R are also popular languages for analytics, offering packages for data manipulation, statistics, and visualisation.

Other tools include Tableau for visualisation, Apache Hadoop and Spark for data processing, and TensorFlow for machine learning applications. Each tool has its strengths and weaknesses, and the choice often comes down to the specific requirements of the task at hand.

4.3. Predictive and Prescriptive Analytics

Predictive and prescriptive analytics represent the advanced stages of data integration. Predictive analytics utilizes algorithms and machine learning techniques to estimate future outcomes, while prescriptive analytics suggests actions you can take to affect those outcomes.

Think of it as the difference between a weather forecast and an umbrella recommendation. Predictive analytics might tell you there's an 80% chance of rain tomorrow (a future outcome), while prescriptive analytics will tell you to carry an umbrella (a recommended action).

4.4. The Beauty of Visualization

Data visualization is another critical component of data analytics. At times, the most elegant solution to a data-heavy problem is the simplest one: a map, a pie-chart, a simple line graph. These visual expressions can summarize vast amounts of complex data and express it in a form that is intuitive and clear. This is an art in itself, quickly communicating information in a format that's easy to understand and digest.

4.5. Ethics and Data Analytics

In the digital age, questions of privacy, confidentiality, and misuse of data are more pertinent than ever. As data professionals, it is essential to implement ethical standards and ensure data protection law compliance. Data analytics should always aim for the advancement of society, never to cause harm or infringe upon people's rights.

4.6. Conclusion: Data Analytics, a Game Changer

Indeed, data analytics has become an integral part of our modern economy. It's enriching businesses, improving decision-making processes, and even reshaping industries. Moreover, it's helping us predict and shape the future, offering immense value to the public and private sectors alike.

As the world produces more data, the need for data analytics will continue to grow. It is an art and a science, depending on technical prowess and creative thought to turn raw data into valuable insights.

The age of big data has only just begun, and it's poised to transform our world in ways that are yet to be imagined. Whether you're a casual observer or knee-deep in this field, understanding data analytics is an essential part of navigating our data-driven future. Hence, it's rightly said, "Knowing is not sufficient; it's time to understand."

Chapter 5. How Big Data is Shaping Businesses

Business dynamics across sectors are being redefined by the transformative implications of big data. The vast datasets generated from numerous online and offline activities carry unprecedented opportunities for understandings deep narratives beneath surface-level patterns, thereby informing strategic directions and decisions.

5.1. The Genesis of Big Data in Business

The narrative of massive data influencing businesses began with the advent of the internet and digital revolution. Companies started accumulating data from various sources, such as online browsing patterns, customer interactions, transactions, and more. Earlier, they had limited channels for data collection, such as physical surveys and personal interactions, which only scratched the surface. Today, the breadth and depth of data available have opened up avenues to deep-dive into uncharted terrains of business intelligence.

5.2. Confluence of Technology and Data

The birth of Big Data is attributable to the confluence of technologies that facilitate its generation, storage, processing, and utilization. High-speed internet, social media, and IoT devices have accelerated data generation, while cloud computing and storage technologies allow for its safekeeping. Sophisticated software and advanced analytics tools have evolved to process these chunky data, extracting meaningful insights for businesses.

5.3. Understanding Customers Through Big Data

Big Data enables a granular understanding of customer behaviors and preferences. Companies can track browsing patterns, purchase histories, social media interactions, and other touchpoints to create a holistic customer profile. This data-driven understanding helps businesses tailor products, services, and marketing strategies to individual customer preferences, drastically enhancing their experience and deepening customer relationships.

5.4. Big Data for Business Strategy and Decision Making

Data-driven insights contribute significantly to business strategy and decision-making. They provide cues for potential market threats and opportunities, competitive strategies, customer sentiment, efficiency improvements, and more. By leveraging Big Data, companies can pivot their strategies quickly in response to changes in market dynamics or customer behavior.

5.5. Big Data for Operational Efficiency

Big Data analytics helps businesses streamline operations and enhance productivity. Businesses can identify patterns in their operational data to spot inefficiencies and bottlenecks. Predictive analytics can forecast future operational issues, allowing for proactive solutions. This results in cost savings, faster delivery times, and improved quality.

5.6. Challenges in Harnessing Big Data

The road to Big Data analytics isn't free from challenges. Data privacy and security concerns loom large. Compliance with data protection regulations is a fundamental concern. Furthermore, the capabilities required to harness Big Data—resources, technology, and skills—can be substantial.

The ability to filter out noise from the massive datasets and derive meaningful insights is a task of vast complexity. The quality and reliability of data are other key challenges. However, advancements in technology, such as AI, machine learning, and cloud computing, are steadily equipping businesses to overcome these challenges.

5.7. The Future of Big Data in Business

Big Data is more than a passing trend, indicative of its upward trajectory in global business. With advancements in AI and machine learning, the application spectrum of big data is set to expand further, from personalized marketing strategies to AI-driven innovation.

Nevertheless, the evolving regulatory landscape and growing demands from customers for transparency and ethical data use will shape how businesses harness big data. Despite the challenges, big data's future in business seems optimistic, offering breakthrough capabilities and transformative potential.

In closure, the era of big data is a powerful and encouraging testament to the ever-evolving dimensions of technology and its sojourn with business. Data and technology orchestrate a remarkable symphony that is setting new trends in business practices, promising a rewarding ally in the journey towards the future.

Chapter 6. Big Data and Public Policy: Towards a Data-Driven Society

Data is undeniably participating in the reshaping of public policy, leading institutions, both public and private, to increasingly rely on data and analytics to inform decision-making. The crossroads of data and public policy is shaping a new era, pushing us towards a society that is data-driven. Its implementation is being woven into the fabric of every sector, from demography to education, to healthcare and economics.

6.1. The Data Revolution

The digital age has given rise to enormous quantities of data. With the advent of technologies such as IoT (Internet of Things), smartphones, and social media, data generation is mutating, expanding faster than ever. The IDC Digital Universe Study predicts the data sphere will reach 175 zettabytes by 2025, and this data is being mined for insights that can help in understanding the world and driving strategic decisions in an accurately responsive manner.

6.2. Technology as a Policy Tool

Policy decisions are influenced by computing power and algorithmic advancements, making big data analytics a potent policy tool. Policy planning and implementation are being revamped as programming is enabling the collection, processing, and interpretation of large datasets in real time.

Machine learning algorithms are letting us identify patterns and trends, thus empowering policy-makers. For instance, predictive policing uses data analysis to predict potential criminal activity, allowing for preventive measures. In healthcare, predictive analytics aid in alerting about potential outbreaks, aiding proactive disease control initiatives. Thus, technology is operating as an evidence-based policy tool with impactful outcomes.

6.3. public policy and Big Data

Public policy is capitalizing on the data revolution by leveraging big data to guide policy shaping. Such practices involve understanding demographics and societal trends, predicting potential issues and their outcomes, and implementing preventive measures with unprecedented precision.

6.4. The Power of Predictive Analytics

Predictive analytics is proving a game-changer in public policy. By using historical data, algorithms can forecast future probability events. Policymakers can monitor these predictions and use them to shape our society. For instance, by recognizing patterns in economic data, an impending recession can be detected, preparing the government to mitigate adverse effects. Similarly, data can predict demographic changes affecting issues like immigration, health, or urban planning, helping in proactive policy making.

6.5. The Role of Data Visualization

With the complexity of big data, how this data is communicated is as equally important as the data itself. Data visualization has evolved as a vital discipline to make data-driven decisions accessible to policy-makers and the public. Infographics, interactive graphs, heat maps, and other visual tools enable decision-makers to understand patterns, trends, and correlations that might go unnoticed in text-based data, thereby facilitating informed policy decisions.

6.6. Challenges and Ethical Considerations

However, with potential comes challenges. The misuse of data can lead to privacy infringement, data bias can taint insights, and the digital divide can marginalize non-digital natives. It's essential that as we move towards a data-driven society, ethical guidelines and legislation keep pace with technology advancements.

Data privacy is a growing concern. The collection and use of data should not encroach on an individual's privacy rights. Measures need to be in place to protect sensitive personally identifiable information (PII).

Data quality and bias pose other major challenges. If the collected data is not representative or is biased, it will influence the resulting policies. Therefore, ensuring that the data is of high quality and unbiased is paramount.

6.7. Democratization of Data

As we continue our navigation through this data-driven era, data democratization – making data accessible to everyone, irrespective of skillset – is gaining momentum. If we are to be a truly participatory democracy, comprehending data and utilizing it should not be the power of a few but the empowerment of all, enhancing the quality of public discourse and collective decision-making. It's not just about administrators using data to make policies but about citizens using data to hold those administrators accountable.

6.8. Conclusion

As we embark on the journey towards a data-driven society, the adoption of big data in public policy is opening new vistas for shaping a responsive and enlightened society. While challenges persist, the rewards are substantial. As we navigate this path, it's crucial to ensure durability, usability, inclusivity, and safeguard ethical considerations. This will enable a digital society that is not only informed by data but also protective of our values, strengthening our democratic institutions in an ever-evolving digital landscape.

Chapter 7. Transforming Health: The Power of Big Data in Medicine

In the era of information overload, the medical field is not an outlier. This increase in patient data, clinical studies, medication-related information, and hospital management statistics presents an opportunity for substantial advancement to a sector that is often seen as lagging in incorporating modern technology. By leveraging advanced analytics, the healthcare industry can transform these volumes of data into actionable insights, inevitably improving patient outcomes.

7.1. Usage of Big Data in Medicine

Big data refers to the massive amount of information that traditional data processing systems cannot handle because of its variety, velocity, volume, and veracity. Encompassing data from both structured and unstructured sources, the application of big data in the healthcare sector can range from predictive modeling to electronic health records (EHRs), genomics, and even wearable device data.

In medicine, leveraging big data considerably augments the foundation of knowledge as the variety of data sources capture a wider range of patient information. Electronic Health Records or EHRs, as some describe, hold a gold mine of health data. By gathering insights from these datasets, predictive analytics can warn medical staff about potential health complications ahead of time, allowing for preventative measures to be established.

Additionally, medical research is a fundamental area where big data shows significant potential. Clinical trials, by their nature, generate vast amounts of data. The relentless assessment and analysis of this data can lead to more in-depth understanding of diseases, ultimately allowing medical professionals to discover and validate novel treatment methods quicker.

7.2. Big Data Analytics for Precision Medicine

Precision medicine represents a paradigm shift from the one-size-fits-all standard of care to individually tailored treatments. It emphasizes the customization of healthcare, considering individual variability in genes, environment, and lifestyle, to offer the most apt treatment plan per person.

Big data analytics is a crucial tool in realizing the potential of precision medicine. When machine learning algorithms access big data sources, such as genomic sequence data and digital medical records, they identify patterns and correlations which enable the prediction of an individual's susceptibility to diseases, or how they may respond to treatments. For instance, a genetic mutation might indicate an increased risk of certain types of cancer, enabling proactive preventative treatment tailored to individual genetic profiles.

7.3. The Role of Wearable Devices and Internet of Things

The Internet of Things (IoT) and wearable technologies play a pivotal role in personal health monitoring, contributing to the proliferation of medical big data. The devices, which can range from smartwatches to sophisticated implanted sensors, can monitor a range of health indicators like heart rate, blood pressure, and glucose levels, providing valuable real-time data.

This flood of data from wearable devices can be integrated with patient health records to create an extensive and continuously updated health profile for each individual. Big data analytics can then process this information to derive meaningful insights for healthcare providers.

7.4. Implications for Hospital Management

Big data can help optimize hospital operations, resulting in improved patient care and cost reductions. It allows for proficient integrity checks, facilitating proactive detection and correction of errors in patient care, staffing, and billing.

Analytics can also be used for patient scheduling, considering historical data from patient appointments to predict no-shows or late arrivals. By managing their resources more efficiently, healthcare institutions can improve their response to patient care demands and minimize patient waiting time.

7.5. The Importance of Integrating Data

Despite the promises of big data, the successful extraction of actionable insights from a vast amount of healthcare data still faces significant hurdles. Integration poses a particular challenge.

Most healthcare data is stored in isolated datasets that do not communicate with each other. For example, a patient's pharmacy records might be stored separately from their hospital records, so it becomes a challenge to get a comprehensive understanding of a patient's health. Therefore, methods to easily and securely integrate these types of data are a necessity.

7.6. Challenges of Big Data

Privacy and security represent critical challenges in the application of big data in healthcare. The balance between sharing and protecting sensitive health data for better care delivery is a pivotal consideration.

Moreover, the requirements for storage, processing, and analysis of big data are beyond the current capacity of many healthcare organizations. Institutions must continuously upgrade their IT infrastructure to handle the volume and speed of incoming data.

Despite these challenges, big data offers numerous avenues for healthcare innovation. It facilitates improvements in patient care, transforms diagnoses and treatment plans, encourages proactive health management, and influences hospital operations. The era of big data in medicine is just beginning, promising to shape the future of healthcare in ways we may not yet perceive. The power of data, when harnessed effectively, can truly revolutionize medicine.

Chapter 8. Big Data and Personalized Education: A New Era of Learning

Educational processes have undergone a radical transformation with the infusion of technology. Big data has started playing a pivotal role in reshaping the landscape, inspiring improvements and innovations. Perhaps one of the most intriguing applications of big data lies in personalizing education, setting the foundation for a new era of learning.

8.1. The Matrix: Big Data in Education

Big data in education refers to the large volumes of information created by students and educators in various forms: digital content, online assessments, performance tracking, and even social interactions. By harnessing this massive, diverse, and rapidly growing data pool, we're beginning to uncover unprecedented insights about learning behaviors, educational methodologies, and student outcomes.

Traditionally, learning has been a somewhat static process, with educators using the same materials and techniques for every student. This one-size-fits-all approach has been recognized as less effective, as it fails to cater to individual learning styles and paces.

The introduction of big data analytics into education can fine-tune this process, making it a dynamic, student-focused experience. We unlock the ability to identify patterns and make predictions accurately, which allows for increasingly informed decision-making about educational practices and policies.

8.2. A Look at Personalized Learning

Personalized learning, as the name suggests, involves adjusting educational content and experiences to meet the unique needs of individual learners. This doesn't merely refer to academic abilities – but also encompasses a student's interests, goals, and preferred learning strategies.

The shift towards this educational model signifies a realization that learning is not a linear process, and that every student is unique. Understanding these intricacies necessitates a detailed, data-driven approach. Enter big data – the key that unlocks truly personalized education.

Big data analytics provides the detailed insights necessary for educators to create personalized learning paths. Adaptive learning software, empowered by big data, is instrumental in providing students with personalized content at their own pace and according to their preferred learning style.

8.3. Assessing the Impact: Outcomes of Personalized Education

The impact of personalized learning facilitated by big data is monumental. It leads to more engaged learners, improved educational outcomes, and a more inclusive education system.

When learning is adapted to a student's pace, they are less likely to lose interest or become overwhelmed. They can spend more time on challenging concepts and skip over those they've already mastered. Furthermore, by injecting personalized interests into curriculum, students are more likely to be engaged in their learning.

From an outcomes perspective, personalizing education allows for individualized assessment – a necessary shift from the traditional model's uniform evaluation styles. These assessments can provide a more detailed understanding of a student's progress and areas that need improvement, thereby creating a more holistic view of educational achievement.

8.4. Ethical Considerations: Privacy & Big Data

Despite the numerous benefits, integrating big data in education comes with significant ethical considerations, mainly circled around privacy issues. With increased data collection, there's the potential for misuse or even breaches of sensitive student information.

As we continue to explore and expand the role of big data in education, it's crucial to establish stringent data governance practices, including well-defined policies around data collection, storage, usage, and sharing. Similarly, there must be robust measures to safeguard this data and ensure compliance with privacy laws.

8.5. Big Data: The Power to Transform

In conclusion, big data offers the power to transform education as we know it. Utilizing this power paves the way for more personalized, efficient, and inclusive learning solutions where each student's unique traits are considered. While the road may involve traversing ethical dilemmas, with careful navigation, it's a pathway that leads to a new era of learning, one characterized by personalized education.

Continuing to harness the potential of big data in education can result in revolutionary changes, affirming the impact of data analytics on our society. But remember, though knowing is the first step, understanding is the key – and it's understanding that big data promotes in the educational landscape.

Chapter 9. Big Data Beyond Borders: International Implications

In the context of a globalized world, big data takes on an international character. Not confined by geographic borders, it flows wherever digital networks reach. The phenomenon of big data crossing borders has far-reaching implications from business strategies to policy making and legal frameworks.

9.1. The Role of Big Data in Globalization

Big data plays an increasingly pivotal role in the globalization process. Its use can shape market trends, drive international business decisions, and even influence geopolitical strategies. Technological advancements make it possible to collect, store, and process vast amounts of data across vast distances, quickly and efficiently. Companies can now analyze market trends and customer behavior in real-time, informing strategic decisions that span continents, while governments can leverage big data to guide policy and shape international relations.

9.2. International Business and Big Data

International business, characterized by its cross-border operations, heavily relies on big data analytics. Multinational corporations derive valuable insights from analyzing the massive datasets they collect globally. Whether it's predicting consumer behavior, optimizing supply chain logistics or identifying opportunities for expansion, big data delivers critical inputs for decision-making.

However, the international aspect also introduces complexities. Varieties in data protection laws, cultural nuances affecting data interpretation, and the logistical challenges of managing data across different regions complicate the data analytics process. Companies need to navigate these complexities to fully harness the potential of big data.

9.3. Big Data and Policy Making

At the policy level, big data offers a rich resource for governments to base their decisions upon. It provides detailed insights on a range of issues, from population health trends to economic indicators. These can guide policies designed to enhance societal welfare and economic prosperity.

On the international stage, big data can facilitate improved understanding and cooperation between nations. It serves as an objective basis for international agreements and treaties. Policymakers can harness big data for cross-border collaborations on issues like global health, climate change, and cybersecurity.

Yet, the cross-border flow of big data also raises issues around data sovereignty, security, privacy, and ethics, which need addressing in international policy discussions.

9.4. Legal Implications of Big Data Across Borders

The legal landscape is still catching up with the unprecedented challenges posed by big data. There is a pressing need for concrete international legal frameworks and agreements to govern the cross-border flow and use of big data.

Data protection laws vary significantly across countries. While Europe's General Data Protection Regulation (GDPR) imposes tight restrictions on data collection and use, other regions might have less stringent rules. Companies operating internationally must comply with this multitude of laws, making business operations complex.

Privacy is another major concern as big data often involves personal information. There are calls for more robust international privacy regulations to safeguard citizens' rights while not hindering the free flow of data.

Finally, there is the challenge of enforcing legal rules and adjudicating disputes in the realm of big data. Digital realms do not respect geographic borders, and this can lead to jurisdictional issues that are difficult to resolve.

9.5. The Future: Towards a Data-Driven World

As digital connectivity deepens and data analytics technology advances, the role of big data in international contexts will continue to grow. It is poised to play an increasingly central role in the global economy, driving innovation and competitiveness. Yet, the journey is not without challenges. Clearer policies, robust legal frameworks, and international cooperation will be paramount to harness this potential fully.

The future needs a cross-border and multi-disciplinary dialogue. This will ensure that the world reaps the numerous benefits of big data, while upholding core values such as privacy, security, and fairness. As we step into an increasingly interconnected and data-driven world, there are both obligations and opportunities for businesses, governments, and individuals alike.

Chapter 10. Concerns and Challenges: Ethics in the Era of Big Data

As we stride into the forefront of the big data era, it becomes imperative to grapple with the ethical dilemmas it presents. Unbounded potential offered by this data revolution also brings with it a baggage of concerns and challenges that need to be acknowledged and addressed.

10.1. Big Data and Privacy Concerns

The vast reservoirs of data being collected today can indeed help resolve countless mysteries and steer us towards an improved future. However, data privacy looms large as one of the most pressing ethical issues. Personal data can reveal a myriad of information about an individual, including sensitive details about daily life, interests, behavior, and health status, among others. Consumer databases crammed with such information, if misused or mishandled, can lead to intrusive violations of privacy.

10.2. Intrusiveness and Informed Consent

Anchored to this privacy debate is the concern of intrusiveness. Businesses often pry into the lives of consumers under the guise of customizing experiences and optimizing services. While in principle, it seems appealing, in practice, it can lead to intrusive observations. People are often oblivious to the extent their data could be mined and the insights that could be drawn from it. Informed consent, thus, becomes a concern. Many users unknowingly agree to share vast amounts of information while navigating dense terms and conditions of service agreements.

10.3. Bias and Discrimination

Big Data doesn't exist in a vacuum. It is a reflection of our society, including its biases and prejudices. If not treated appropriately, these biases can get embedded into the algorithms and models built upon this data, leading to systematized discrimination. Models built on biased data can disproportionately affect certain demographics, leading to concerns over fairness, justice, and discrimination. Addressing these issues requires the development and employment of fair and transparent modelling practices.

10.4. Data Quality and Veracity

The quantity of data is increasing exponentially, but the same cannot be assured for quality and veracity. The challenge lies in distinguishing between high-quality, useful data and low-quality, misleading or outdated data. Poor data quality compromises the accuracy and reliability of insights, leading to misguided decision-making. In the era of fake news and misinformation, it is paramount to ensure the integrity and accuracy of data.

10.5. Data Ownership and Governance

As we generate and accumulate vast amounts of data, the question of who owns this data becomes pertinent. The current landscape is marked by a power imbalance, where data brokers monopolize profits off people's personal data while the subjects of this information remain largely uncompensated. There is a need for a robust governance structure that demarcates clear rules for data ownership, control, and usage while ensuring fair compensation.

10.6. The Inevitability of Security Breaches

While cybersecurity measures have been ramped up, the likelihood of security breaches still looms. The sheer scale of data being processed and stored increases exposure to potential breaches. A single breach could lead to catastrophic consequences, underscoring the need for stringent data protection protocols.

10.7. Accountability and Transparency

The complexity and opacity of machine learning algorithms and analytical models pose challenges to accountability. If an algorithm built on big data makes a decision, it may be challenging to understand how and why that decision was made. Transparent operational frameworks are needed to ensure that bad decisions do not get hidden behind the inscrutability of complex models.

10.8. The Balance between Utility and Misuse

The quintessential challenge in this big data era lies in striking that delicate balance between harnessing its immense potential and preventing its misuse. Unregulated practices and an unethical use of data can lead to dystopian scenarios, undermining the fabric of our society.

We stand on the brink of a significant societal shift, driven by big data. By keeping ethics as a guiding compass, it becomes possible to navigate this uncharted terrain, leveraging big data's potential while limiting its perils. The collective responsibility lies upon us - data scientists, policymakers, businesses, and end consumers - to foster a fruitful, ethical transition into the era of big data. It's time to move beyond the mere collection and analysis of data, towards creating a moral framework grounded in respect for individual rights and societal wellbeing.

Chapter 11. The Future of Big Data: Predictions and Implications

The explosion of data, which constitutes the very fabric of an increasingly complex interrelated global system, cannot be overstated. Drawing from numerous sources such as the Internet of Things (IoT), machine learning algorithms, social media feeds, and myriad others, big data's size, complexity, and growth rate dwarf anything known before. Harnessing these massive troves of data has transformative potential, suggesting new business and policy models, fostering innovation, and enhancing decision-making processes. This promises an exciting future, yes, but also imposes an undeniable obligation on us to understand its implications.

11.1. The Dawn of Data-driven Decision Making

Consider the potential for data-driven decision making in shaping the future. As our ability to collect, store, and analyze data improves, the gap between data-rich and data-poor organizations will widen dramatically. From healthcare to retail, manufacturing to finance, those able to harness the bounty of data will drive innovation and improve outcomes, while those unable to adapt will lag.

Data-driven decision makers will leverage continuously updated datasets with millions or even billions of data points. They will draw on data-driven insights more efficiently and accurately than ever before. This kind of granular insight will transform strategic decision making. The ability to examine microtrends and behavioral patterns across large populations enables predictive modeling, leading to substantial efficiency and productivity gains.

11.2. The Ascendency of Artificial Intelligence

Artificial Intelligence (AI) and machine learning (ML), two of the most transformative technologies of our era, owe their potential largely to data availability. These technologies use sophisticated algorithms to 'learn' from data and make independent decisions.

AI's capacity to process vast amounts of data and predict outcomes will grow synergistically with big data. This will lead to the development of more refined predictive algorithms. Consequently, expectation is that there will be a proliferation of AI-based systems across industries. Whether it be in managing supply chains, diagnosing illnesses, or optimizing energy use, AI will increasingly underpin the operations of society.

11.3. Challenges: Privacy and Security

The future of big data brings not only benefits but significant challenges, chief among them are privacy and security concerns. With greater collection and analysis of data, the opportunities for misuse or unintended consequences also increase. Privacy is a fundamental human right, but how does it coalesce with the need for data in an interconnected world? The development of robust, universally applicable privacy policies is integral to our future.

Similarly, security breaches pose a serious threat. Many big data users, especially in the private sector, hold sensitive information. The increasing sophistication of cyberattacks heightens the need for robust data protection strategies and the development of advanced security technologies.

11.4. Mitigating the Digital Divide

A future increasingly reliant on big data may exacerbate social inequalities, creating a digital divide. As the value of data grows, those with limited access to digital resources may become further marginalized.

Thus, mitigating the digital divide's potential negative effects becomes urgent. Ensuring widespread access to digital resources and fostering digital literacy are steps towards minimizing the digital divide. Policies geared toward creating inclusive digital societies are critical in the Age of Big Data.

11.5. Ethical Use of Data

Questions about the ethical use of data arise as data becomes increasingly influential in decision-making. Who gets to decide how data should be used? And what are the ethical considerations in doing predictive analytics? Ethical guidelines that straddle the boundary between data utility and respect for individual rights will dictate the course of big data's future.

11.6. The Need For Legislation And Regulation

Given the far-reaching implications of big data, it seems necessary and reasonable for countries to assess the adequacy of their existing legal and regulatory frameworks pertaining to data management, security and personal privacy protections. Indeed, the global ubiquity of data warrants a comprehensive regulatory framework that considers differing cultural, social and economic contexts.

11.7. Road Ahead: Embrace the Change

The future of big data promises immense growth propelled by technological advancements, sophisticated analytics, and burgeoning AI capabilities. We must prepare ourselves to harness this potential. By adopting a forward-looking approach and being cognizant of the ethical, social, and economic implications, organizations and societies can navigate this new data-infused landscape confidently and effectively. As we move forward, let us not just be observers at the dawn of the Age of Big Data, but active participants shaping the destiny of our increasingly interconnected society.